Kenya

A land of contrast

Contents

His Excellency the President of the Republic of Kenya, Mzee Jomo Kenyatta.

Kenya's History

Although Kenya is one of the world's most modern developing countries its history dates back many thousand of years to the Stone and Iron Ages when most parts of the country were inhabited by man as evidenced by archaeological objects which have been excavated in many places.

The first intruders at the Kenya Coast were the Islamic Arabs in the 9th century A.D. who settled in the Lamu area and then spread out southwards. They were later followed by the Europeans, starting with the Portuguese. The ruins of Gedi in Malindi and Fort Jesus on the Island of Mombasa are landmarks of that historical period.

The outside world knew very little about Kenya's hinterland until European explorers, missionaries and traders too began to penetrate and settle in the country.

Between 1895 and 1901 the British Government built a railway from Mombasa to Kisumu on the shores of Lake Victoria with the aim of establishing permanent communications with Uganda. The British used a great deal of force to assert their presence and many tribesmen were killed and their property destroyed as they resisted the white man's intrusion. These "Wars of Pacification" ended in 1908.

In 1902 Kenya was declared a British Protectorate. This sparked off a long series of land-grabbing activities which dis-possessed indigenous people on the pain of death and the land allocated to white settlers. This policy continued for more than 50 years. Land was leased to the farmers for 999 years. Kenya was declared a British colony in 1920.

When the legislative Council was inaugurated in 1907 the indigenous people had no representation while the 600 odd settlers in the country were well represented.

Africans suffered in many ways. During the first world war about 165,000 were conscripted to serve as carriers and at least 50,000 of them perished in the jungle because of undernourishment, disease and exhaustion.

After the war young African men and women were being rounded to work for European farmers as forced labour.

These incursions into the civil liberties of the African people were fermenting conflicts which were to erupt later.

A group of Africans protesting against forced labour were gunned down in Nairobi during the "Harry Thuku Affair" in 1922.

Although such organisations as the Kikuyu Central Association and the Kavirondo Taxpayers Welfare Association tried to wrestle basic human rights from the colonialist, all channels were closed.

This was the time when Mzee Kenyatta—Kenya's President, came to the front line of the political battle. He continued this fight for Africans' rights in Britain for many years.

During the World War II African political leaders were banished to remote areas to ensure that African youths were lured to fight the whiteman's war.

It was only in October 1944 that the first African was nominated as a Member of the Legislative Council. African masses then organised to found a countrywide party—Kenya African Union of which Mzee Jomo Kenyatta became President in 1947. Since then Kenya African endeavours to attain political freedom never relaxed. During seven years of "The Emergency" (1952-59) thousands of indigenous people were killed; others suffered in prisons and detention camps.

The first African elections were held in March 1957 after which time changes in the composition of Kenya Government came steadily. By 1960 the Legislative Council had an African majority-33 of the 53 constituency seats for the first time in Kenya's history.

At the end of all this concerted struggle, the Kenya African National Union (KANU) led by Jomo Kenyatta, after his release from imprisonment and detention in August 1961, attained independence for

Kenya on 12th December, 1963. Kenya was declared a Republic exactly a year later.

Kenya's Constitution

Kenya achieved internal selfgovernment on 1st June, 1963, and became an independent sovereign state on 12th December, 1963. On the first anniversary of independence, Kenya became a Republic.

The Republic Constitution declares Kenya to be a Sovereign Republic and makes provision regarding citizenship, protection of the fundamental rights and freedoms of the individual, the President, the Cabinet and Parliament, the Judiciary, the Judical Service Commission and the courts, the Public Service Commission, and the safeguarding of Trust Land.

The President is the Head of State and Commander-in-chief of the Kenya Armed Forces. He is aided and advised by a Cabinet of Ministers who are appointed by him, from among the Members of Parliament. The Attorney-General is also a member of the Cabinet.

The President, who must be a member of the National Assembly and not less than 35 years of age, is normally elected at the General Election which follows a dissolution of Parliament.

Parliament must be dissolved every five years but may be dissolved sooner by the President. At a General Election a candidate for President shall be nominated by each political party in the General Election. He must be supported by not less than one thousand persons registered as voters in elections to the National Assembly.

Candidates for National Assembly elections, unless nominated unopposed, are selected at party preliminary elections at which any registered voter who declares himself to be a member or supporter of the party may vote. As only one political party exists, no polling takes place at Parliamentary or Presidential elections, but only at preliminary elections.

Parliament consists of a single chamber, called the National Assembly. It has

158 elected members (including the President), 12 members nominated by the President, and two *ex officio* members, the Speaker (elected by the National Assembly), and the Attorney-General (a civil servant appointed by the President). The National Assembly also elects one of its members as Deputy Speaker. An elected or nominated member must be a Kenya Citizen of not less than 21 years of age and must be registered as a voter.

In the Republican Constitution executive and legislative powers are divided so as to give effect to three main principles; namely that strong national leadership should exist and be apparent to the people, that the President and his cabinet should be collectively responsible to Parliament, and that Parliament should be supreme.

Strong national leadership is assured by the election of the executive President, who with his Cabinet governs with the support of the majority in Parliament. The supremacy of Parliament is assured in that the President must resign or dissolve Parliament if he cannot command its support, in that Parliament is the only law-making body and in that the control of public finance is exercised by Parliament.

Area and Location

The Republic of Kenya is approximately 225,000 square miles (582,647 square kilometres) in size, and lies across the Equator, on the eastern seaboard of Africa.

The Indian Ocean coastline, stretching from the Somalia border in the north to Tanzania in the South, is 380 miles (608 km.) long. The Republic of Somalia lies to the east of Kenya, Ethiopia lies to the north, Tanzania to the south and Uganda to the west.

Kenya is made up of seven provinces. These are: Coast, Central, Rift Valley, Nyanza, Western, North-Eastern, Eastern and Nairobi area.

Population

The analysis of the 1969 Census indicates that the crude birth and death rates for Kenya for the period immediately proceeding the 1969 census were respectively 50 and 17 per thousand, giving a rate of population increase of 3.3 per cent per annun. The expectation of life at birth was estimated at 51 and 47 years for females and males respectively. It is very likely that these indices have changed since the analysis of 1969 Census, although the degree of change is not ascertained yet. The mid-year population for 1974 was estimated at 12,912 thousands.

Climate

The altitude in Kenya largely governs the climate and the land above 5,000 feet enjoys a temperate climate with fairly good rainfall. Being on the Equator however, there are no marked seasonal changes and, for most parts of the country there are two rainy seasons on the high ground to the east of the Rift (i.e. around Nairobi): there are "long rains" (March to May) and the "short rains" (November to December).

While the Coastal strip and Mombasa have a hot, humid climate, the trade winds which blow in from the sea during most of the year keep the temperature from soaring above the 100 degrees Fahrenheit. Rarely is the mean maximum temperature in Mombasa above 90 degrees Fahrenheit, the hottest months being February and March. July and August are the coolest months on the coast, the mean minimum temperature being about 68.5 degrees Fahrenheit.

Temperatures in Nairobi vary from a mean maximum of 82 degrees (February) to mean minimum of about 52 degrees (June/July). Nakuru temperatures vary from 85 degrees down to 45 degrees. Eldoret from 78 degrees to 45 degrees and Kisumu from 87 degrees to 60 degrees.

While the highland and the Lake Victoria region of

Nyanza enjoy good rainfall reaching as much as 80 inches a year at Kericho, the greatest part of the North Eastern Province has little or no rainfall at all. Other fairly dry areas include Masailand, Kitui and coastal hinterland where the year's total varies between 10 inches and 20 inches.

Topography

From the hot, humid coastal belt, the land rises gradually inland through dry bush country (the Nyika) to the Savannah grasslands and the high land, where rainfall is plentiful. Kenya is cut by the Great Rift Valley which runs from north to south between 2,000 feet (610 metres) and 3,000 feet (914 metres) below the country on both sides, and varies in depth. A considerable area of the country is ideal for high-potential mixed farming in which temperate crops can be grown and mixed farming is advocated. In the drier areas some four fifths of the area is ideal range land.

On the western rim of the Rift Valley the land slopes down towards Lake Victoria and the Uganda border. The central part of Kenya is extremely mountainous, but the vast expanse of the North-Eastern Province varies from featureless desert in the east to the more rugged Turkana, west of Lake Rudolf (now Lake Turkana).

LAKES

Lake Turkana, an alkaline lake which lies in the Rift Valley, stretches for 180 miles up to the Ethiopian border. It is the largest lake wholly within Kenya (2,473 square kilometres), although Lake Victoria 24,300 square miles, (62,937 square kilometres) the largest lake in Africa and second largest in the world, falls partly within Kenya.

The smaller Kenya lakes include Lake Naivasha, 81 square miles, (210 square kilometres), Baringo, 50 square miles, (129 square kilometres), Hannington (now Bogoria) 13 square miles, (34 square kilometres), Nakuru 20 square miles, (52 square kilometres) and Elementaita 7 square miles, (21 square

8

kilometres). Most of these lakes are fairly shallow and alkaline, supporting large populations of flamingoes and other birds.

Lake Magadi lying in the Rift Valley near the Tanzania border, is an important source of soda ash and salt. Lake Amboseli within the Amboseli Game Reserve, is no longer a permanent lake, but fills up after heavy rains.

Only Lake Victoria has any commercial craft, although Lake Turkana is used by fishing boats, as are Baringo and Naivasha.

RIVERS

The Tana is Kenya's largest river, draining off the slopes of Mt. Kenya and the Aberdare Range into the Indian Ocean to the north of Mombasa. It is liable to flooding and the people who live among the lower reaches are marooned for several weeks each year. It is only navigable by small crafts.

Smaller rivers include the Athi river, which becomes the Galana and then Sabaki nearer the coast. Into this flows the Tsavo River.

The Uaso Nyiro, which rises in the Aberdares and Mt. Kenya, flows into the fringe of the North Eastern Province to disappear in the vast Lorian Swamp. The Turkwell flows north east from Mt. Elgon and down the Rift Valley Escarpment into Lake Turkana. Many small rivers empty into Lake Victoria.

MOUNTAINS

Mt. Kenya, a long extinct volcano lying some 100 miles (160 kilometres) northeast of Nairobi is Kenya's highest mountain, reaching 17,058 feet (5,199 metres). It carries not less than 12 glaciers beneath the twin rocks of Batian and Nellion. The snowline is perennial above 15,000 feet.

Mt. Elgon on the Kenya-Uganda border, reaches 14,178 feet, (4,321 metres) and is just below the snowline, although at certain times of the year the summit experiences snowfalls and heavy frosts.

The Aberdares Range, which extends for about 100 miles (160 kilometres) from north to south starting not far from Nairobi, is thickly forested along its slopes. Above this is moorland. Highest point in the

Fort Jesus, Mombasa.

Kilindini Harbour, Mombasa.

The City of Nairobi with Nairobi Hilton in the foreground.

Aberdare Range, is 13,104 feet (3,994 metres).

Although the North-Eastern Province is fairly flat, there are several notable mountain ranges and peaks rising out of the lowlying country, including the Mathews Range, Marsabit Mountain, Mt. Nyiro and Mt. Kulal, near Lake Turkana.

Towns

It is important to note that in quite a few cases, towns include varying portions whose populations are quite rural in character as contrasted with purely urban life.

NAIROBI: It is the capital city and the international centre of Kenya. Most of the commercial, industrial and financial enterprises have their headquarters in Nairobi and is also the commercial hub of the whole of East Africa. It is at an altitude of 5,452 feet and is about mid way between the Indian Ocean and the shores of Lake Victoria. At mid-1974, Nairobi had a projected population of 723,000 persons.

MOMBASA: The second biggest town in Kenya is also the chief port of East Africa and major tourist resort for both the local and overseas visitors. Mombasa's population in 1969 was 247,073 made up of about 187,000 Africans, 39,000 Asians, 16,000 Arabs and 5,000 Europeans. At mid-1974 the total population of Mombasa was projected at 338,600.

KISUMU: Situated at an altitude of 3,725 feet, it is the chief port on Lake Victoria and the third biggest town in Kenya. It is the commercial centre of the growing Nyanza Province and an area providing one of the main sources of grain supply in Kenya. It is linked to Nairobi and the rest of Kenya by a tarmac highway and railway line from Mombasa. In 1969 its population was 110,000 after boundary changes and at mid-1974 it was projected at 146,700.

NAKURU: At an altitude of 6,071 feet, it lies in the Rift Valley some 100 miles north west of Nairobi. It is connected by a major highway and the main railway line with several important towns in Kenya. Of the total population of 50,000 reported in 1969 after its boundary adjustments, 45,000 were Africans. The mid-1974 projection was 64,700 persons.

MERU: It is situated in one of the richest farming areas of Kenya. It is served by a good network of roads and is a fast growing municipality. The municipal boundaries were considerably extended in 1971, resulting in an eleven fold increase in population. At mid-1974, the population was estimated at 61,300.

ELDORET: Its altitude is 6,875 feet and lies on the main road and railway line to Uganda. It is the centre of Uasin Gishu, a busy farming district. Eldoret has become an important educational centre and has a thriving grain-milling industry. In 1969 its population totalled 18,200. The mid-1974 population figure was 36,500.

THIKA: A rapidly expanding town of tremendous industrial potential has overtaken a number of older municipalities in size and importance. It has attracted a number of textile, canning of fruits and vegetables and metalware industries. Its boundary was extended in 1971 and the 1969 adjusted population was 23,000. The population in mid-1974 was 34,300.

NYERI: It lies in the trough between Mount Kenya and the Aberdares at an altitude of 6,200 feet. It is the headquarters of Kenya's Central Province which has a rich agricultural potential. A few miles away from Nyeri Municipality lies the famous game viewing hotels—the Treetops and the Ark which attract large numbers of tourists every year. The 1969 population totalled 24,000 and the mid-1974 figure was projected to be 29,400.

KAKAMEGA: The administrative headquarters for the Western Province is served by main trunk road and is connected to the national electricity grid. Its trading potential is very high and is located in a densely populated area with fertile soil and adequate rainfall which is suitable for the cultivation of a wide range of valuable cash-crops. After the boundary extension of Kakamega Municipality in 1969, the total population was 20,500. In mid-1974 the population equalled 25,700.

KITALE: Located to the East of Mount Elgon at an altitude of 6,200 feet, it is in the midst of rich farmland of Trans-Nzoia district. The district produces coffee, dairy produce, pyrethrum, maize, wheat and some tea. Kitale is linked by not only rail to Eldoret and the main Nairobi-Kakamega railway line but also by a good network of roads leading to Uganda and other parts of Kenya. With boundary extensions, the 1969 population became 13,300 and the mid-1974 population was projected at 18,600 persons.

NANYUKI: It is a busy farming centre situated at the foot of Mount Kenya, at an altitude of 6,389 feet. Near the town is famous Mount Kenya Safari Club. In 1969 the population was 11,600 and by mid-1974 the population projection showed a figure of 15,600 persons.

MALINDI: Malindi is basically a fishing and agricultural service town, but has a rapidly expanding tourist industry which has resulted in its being one of the fastest growing towns in Kenya. In 1969 the population was 10,800 and by mid-1974 the population figure reached 15,100.

KERICHO: It is in the midst of a major tea growing area of Kenya and is an important centre of the tea industry in Kenya. Its population in 1969 was 10,100 and the mid-1974 population totalled 14,200.

EMBU: Embu was upgraded to a municipal status after 1971 and is at present a small town (1969 population 7,700), with only a moderate industrial potential. It is the provincial headquarters for the Eastern Province. The mid-1974 population was projected at 11,900 persons.

FORESTRY:

A wide variety of forest types is found in Kenya varying from the Coastal Mangroves to Coniferous mountain forest, with limited areas of tropical rain forest. Kenya also has the largest area of planted forest in all independent Africa, South of the Sahara. Reserved forest covers almost 16645.5 sq. kilometres, (1,66413.9 ha) which is about 2.8% of total area of Kenya and 2.92% of total land area of Kenya.

Annual production of timber from forests is about 360,000 cubic metres and is expected to rise to about 500,000 cubic metres by the end of 1975. The export of forest products is increasing annually and is expected to be of the order of £8.8 million per annum by the end of 1975.

There are three plywood mills in operation at Sokoro, Elgeyo and Eldoret. The three mills are producing 3.8 million square metres of wood annually. Two similar mills, one at Transmara and the other at North East Mt. Kenya to be constructed soon will add production of plywood to 5.4 million square metres per annum.

A fibre-board factory at Elburgon started production towards the end of 1974 and is expected to produce 700 tons of manufactured fibre board when fully operational. The Webuye pulp and paper mill built at a cost of £17,000,000 started production towards the end of 1974. This mill is the largest consumer of round logs with a capacity of taking in 275,000 cubic metres. The initial production of 45,000 tons of industrial paper is expected to reach 100,000 tons at full production with an annual increase of 10 per cent. This project alone is expected to create jobs for about 4,000 people.

Estimates of future demand for forest products including pulp and paper indicate that the country needs to have planted by 1980 softwood forests covering 142,000 hectares of sawwood, and 20,000 hectares of pulp wood. Between 1974 and 1978 about 40,000 hectares will be planted. To-day about 135,000 hectares of plantation have been established. Clear-felling during this period will amount to about 18,420 hectares.

MINING:

Kenya's mining industry has shown a steady but useful growth over the past few years. In 1973 for example, the total value of mineral production exceeded K£3,700,000 and cement production reached K£7,000,000. The most important product fetching high value was soda (K£2,325,191). Limestone products (K£227,441), mainly from Kajiado and Koru and Carbon Dioxide Gas (K£162,500) from Uplands and Esageri. Fluorspar mining in the Kerio Valley is probably going to take the lead in tonnage and value.

Up to November 1974, fluorspar exports for that year had amounted to K£600,000. Reserves are estimated to be over 10 million tonnes and a concetration plant has just been completed. In 1973 fluorspar valued at K£306,742 was sold mainly overseas and a small proportion went to Bamburi Portland Cement Co. Ltd. for the cement manufacture.

Lead/Silver mining in the Kinangoni area in the Coast Province has continued to show good returns with exports in the last 4 months of 1974 being recorded to the value of K£42,500. The concetration plant has been expanded and will increase product output from the mine.

Gemstone mining continued unabated and during 1974 two new finds of ruby in the Tsavo National Park West and Tsavorite (Green Grosullar Garnet) from the Mgama ridge in the Taita Taveta district were recorded. Exports of the green garnet alone was valued at over K£70,600. Another mineral that showed significant value during 1974 was magnetite (K£98,900).

Oil exploration continued during the year with a record of some nineteen companies operating nine licences. The main work included seismic, geophysical programmes. It is anticipated that a few companies may proceed to drilling test wells within the next six months.

LAND

The total area of Kenya is approximately 582,646

square kilometres which includes part of one of the great lakes of Africa, Lakes Victoria and Turkana, which together with other areas of water comprise 13,393 square kilometres. Also there are over 12,950 square kilometres of forest, including a number of important catchment areas.

Less than 10 per cent of the country enjoys an annual rainfall of 75 centimetres or more, yet this small fraction of land carries the bulk of the country's population. A further 13 per cent of the land receives adequate rainfall for grazing, while some 66 per cent of the land situated mainly in the north and south and the northen part of the Coast Province is arid and unsuitable at present for normal agriculture. Peoples with a traditionally nomadic way of life inhabit these parts of the country, but with the Government's encouragement more stable pattern of land ownership and more efficient methods of agricultural practices are progressively being introduced to the areas.

There are three categories of land ownership in Kenya, namely, Government land, trust land and private freehold land. Government land comprises all the land which, prior to 12th December 1963 when Kenya attained independence, was known as crown land and includes all the urban land within municipalities and townships in the former scheduled areas formerly commonly known as the 'White Highlands'.

Trust land comprises all the land which, prior to 12th December, 1963 when Kenya attained independence was known as Special areas together with certain areas formally known as special reserves, settlement areas and the former Northern Province. It also includes all the urban land within municipalities, townships and trading centres within the special areas commonly known as native land units.

Trust land is vested in the County Council within whose areas of jurisdiction the land is situated. With the exception of the urban land all the other trust land is held in trust for the benefit of the people occupying the land under customary laws.

Private owner freehold land comprises former crown land in respect of which freehold interest was granted by crown in the early years before the 1920's or converted to freehold in 1961 under the 'Conversion of Leases Regulations, 1961'. It also includes agricultural trust land in respect of which individual claims have been fully adjudicated under the 'Land Adjudication Act' and the freehold interest in the land registered under the 'Land Act' and the land in the coastal strip in respect of which individual claims have been adjudicated by a Recorder of Titles under the 'Land Titles Act'.

In due course it will include land in certain areas of the former crown land which have been purchased by the Settlement Fund Trustees and subsequently allocated to settlers under a loan repayment system who have been promised freehold title to their plots after the individual settlers have completed the repayment of their loans.

It is in the Trust land areas that a programme for land consolidation and adjudication has been taking place since 1956. This programme has been placed on an accelerated basis. Its object is to regroup individual holdings of land that previously consisted of small uneconomic fragments, thus providing each land owner with a parcel or parcels of economic size. Elsewhere where fragmentation had not taken place, it determines with certainty the rights of ownership which previously existed under customary tenure. Following consolidation and adjudication of land rights, freehold registered titles to the land are then issued in favour of its owners. Up to the end of 1972 a total of 3,147,116 hectares of land formerly in the Trust land had been fully adjudicated and it is proposed that another 7 million hectares of Trust land, of which 5.5 million hectares will be range land, should be similarly adjudicated in the next five years.

The registration of titles to land will improve agricultural productivity. It reduces land litigation and facilitates the granting of agricultural credit, and will also enable what in the past were Trust Land areas to make a full contribution to the national economy. The laws under which these changes in the Trust Land areas are being achieved are the Land Adjudication Act, the Land Consolidation Act and the Registered Land Act.

Transactions in agricultural land have, for many years in Kenya, been subjected to control, but since independence, land control has been strengthened to prevent uneconomic use of agricultural land, its refragmentation, speculation transactions and the sale of agricultural land to persons who are not Kenya citizens. A comprehensive land control measure known as the Land control Act was introduced in December 1967.

The Constitution, introduced when Kenya was declared a Republic, as well as all subsequent amendments, reaffirmed that all estates, interests or rights in the land which the previous Government had created were confirmed as being validly recognised to the extent they were still subsisting immediately before the constitution came into operation.

The constitution also established a Central Land Board to select agricultural land in the former Scheduled areas once known as the "White Highlands" for the settling of landless and unemployed people on reasonably sized settlement plots with good agricultural potential. The board through its professional valuers, was responsible for assessing the fair value of the land it intended to acquire by agreement with the owners. It was replaced in 1965 by the Settlement Fund Trustees.

After land has been acquired by the Settlement Fund Trustees, it is divided into smallholder units varying from small but economically and agriculturally viable plots up to around 100 acres. These units are granted for agricultural purposes on freehold terms with conditions requiring the new farmers to cultivate the land, build a house, erect a perimeter fence or hedge and generally improve the land. The land is initially granted to the new farmer on payment of legal charges. He is allowed to pay for the land in half-yearly instalments at an interest rate of 6½ per cent per annum.

In 1965, a Special Commissioner was appointed by the Government to look into the problem of squatters, make recommendations on how best the problem could be tackled, and co-ordinated the Government's effort in effecting the recommended and accepted solution. A programme of rehabilitation of the squatters was adopted and continues to include land resettlement in rural areas, rehousing in low-costing houses in the urban areas and employment.

The department of the

Sugar Cane plantation in Nyanza Province.

Smallholder tea garden in Central Province.

Special Commissioner for Squatters was abolished in July 1971, and the remaining work was handed over to the Settlement Department for finalisation.

In Kenya's urban centres, land is alienated for development for apropriate terms of years and all leases issued both by the Government and by county councils contain clauses specifying the use of which the land is to be put, the period during which development is to be completed and the rental reserved under the lease. Urban rentals are revisable where leases for 99 years are issued on the revaluation of the land in the thirty-third and sixty-sixth years of the term.

To achieve uniformity of administration of Government and Trust Land in both agricultural and urban areas, the commissioner of lands is empowered to administer the land both on behalf of the Government and county councils.

Agriculture

The Agricultural Sector is by far the most important in Kenya's economy. Agriculture directly contributes one-third of the gross domestic product, employs three-fourths of the population and supplies most of Kenya's exports. Since independence, production has increased tremendously with gross farm revenue increasing from £52 million to nearly £147 million by 1974. Kenya's agricultural economy is one of the most advanced in Eastern and Central Africa and also one of the most diversified. Virtually every important foodstuff and agricultural commodity is grown or produced in Kenya.

Kenya's most important cash crops are coffee, tea, maize, wheat, pyrethrum, horticultural products and sisal. Coffee is the largest single cash crop, employing approximately 200,000 full and parttime workers. Kenya produces the "Colombian Mild" variety of coffee which is used for flavour blending with other varieties. Because of its high quality, Kenya-grown coffee usually fetches the highest prices on the world market.

Kenya is the largest producer of tea in Africa, and again Kenya tea is known for its high quality. Tea production is fast becoming small-holder dominated, with over 70,000 farmers presently growing tea. The recent construction of a green tea factory will allow Kenya to participate in the vast East Asian tea Market. The small-holder prominence in the tea industry is a result of Government's concerted effort towards fair distribution of wealth for its people leading to more help to small scale farmers to improve their husbandry through the help of extension services accorded to them by Government and through credit facilities given to deserving cases to develop their small-holdings.

Maize is grown on almost every farm in Kenya, as it is the principal foodstuff of the people. Since Kenya is a surplus maize producer, efforts are under way to set up manufacturing and processing industries based on maize. Already, Kenya has sold some 1.6 million bags of maize i.e. 0.16 million metric tons, most of it to the U.K. from its 1972 maize surplus which was causing great strain on its grain rendering it difficult to absorb the 1972/73 bumper maize crop.

Wheat production in

Agricultural Production

PRODUCTS	1963	(Metric Tons) 1972
Coffee	35,800	61,200
Tea	17,000	53,300
Pyrethrum Flowers	5,700	13,800
Cotton	15,300 Bales	29,000 Bales
Horticulture exports	Nil	7,900
Maize	211,600	373,000
Rice	12,400	31,700
Milk Sales	183.4 mill. litres	265.4 mill. litres

Kenya has stabilized at a level sufficient to meet the country's needs. To meet future requirements however, the Government has embarked upon new wheat schemes in Masai Narok districts. These schemes will not only supply the country with needed grain, but will give a steady cash crop income to the present pastoral people in the area. Because Kenya has by tradition to supply wheat to Uganda as well, in 1972 it became necessary to import limited quantities of wheat to guarantee supply to Uganda.

Horticultural production, primarily pineapples, flowers and vegetables has in recent years become a major export industry. Marketing and grading centres are being established throughout the country in an effort to guarantee a steady supply of produce to buyers.

Pyrethrum is used for non-toxic insecticides and Kenya produces 80 per cent of the world's supply of this product. Quality control, and higher pyrethrum-content varieties have enabled Kenya to strongly compete with synthetic products.

Sisal, once one of the top three exports of Kenya has declined in recent years. However, recent higher prices brought on by lower production has allowed the most efficient producers to compete. This commodity is important in as much as it is a dryland crop. Efforts are being made to diversify the use of sisal from its traditional uses of twine and rope to carpets and mats. This is expected to increase demand for sisal.

Kenya also has a large and ever-expanding livestock industry. Most of the country is suitable to ranching and there is an important dairy industry in the higher rainfall areas. Kenya exports large quantities of beef to neighbouring countries, to the Middle East and to Europe. The recent access to the European market followed a vast and successful disease eradication and control effort by the Government.

The dairy industry in Kenya has expanded tremendously in recent years. Dairy products such as milk, butter, cheese and

Wheat harvesting in the highlands.

Dairy Cows in a settlement plot.

ghee are abundant throughout the country, with large amounts also available for export. Pig and poultry production is also sufficient for local needs.

In addition to the principal crop and livestock products mentioned earlier, Kenya also produces large amounts of beans, potatoes, cashewnuts, onions, rice, coconuts, sugar cane, fruit, wattle bark, hides and skins, wool and cotton yearly. Macadamia nuts too are becoming important and plans are underway for a factory for processing macadamia nuts which are a popular item at cocktail parties in countries like America.

Because two-thirds of the country is presently too dry for farming, the Government has in recent years embarked upon large scale irrigation projects throughout the drier sections of the country. These projects upon completion will ensure a better diet, and a higher standard of living for people in these areas.

Education

All sections of the educational services have continued to expand rapidly and improve since the attainment of independence. Good progress has been recorded right from Primary to University level.

Primary education lasts for seven years after which pupils sit for the Certificate of Primary Examination. The Government is committed to doing all it can to achieve the target of universal primary education by 1980. Its first step to reach 75% attendance of school age children by 1974 has been surpassed owing to the introduction of free education in std. I to IV.

In 1963 enrolment in all secondary schools in Kenya was approximately 30,000 pupils. Of this number slightly more than 9,000 were Kenyan Africans. In 1974 the enrolment in all secondary schools in Kenya was over 195,000 of which the vast majority were Kenya Africans. This enormous growth rate was not a result of Government planning alone; of the 195,000 pupils, over 90,000 were in un-aided schools. The Government's original intention was to expand secondary education rapidly and in relatively large schools where up-to-date equipment could be afforded. In 1972, of 53,000 places available in form 1 of secondary schools, just over 23,000 were in schools aided by the Government. The people of Kenya, however, had their own plans. They wanted opportunities for their children to go on to secondary schools and so they built the schools themselves, employed the teachers and set up committees and boards to run them. In no other sphere of social service did the spirit of Harambee reveal itself with more enthusiasm than in the provision of additional secondary schools. In 10 years the people of Kenya built well over 700 schools.

In technical education, as in all other fields, the voluntary and spontaneous effort of the people is beginning to make itself felt. Since 1966 a number of village polytechnics have been started in various parts of Kenya. In 1971 appeals for about 14 colleges of technology, or advanced Institutes of technology were launched. These are intended to specialise in the technical and technological studies associated with production development in different areas.

In order to minimise the problem of unqualified teachers in primary schools the number of trainees has been doubled in the training colleges during the last 10 years. Again with the help of Canadian Technical Assistance a programme of in-service training has been provided to help unqualified teachers to gain a qualification by part-time study, use of radio and correspondence courses and intensive residential courses in holiday time.

The output of secondary teachers was planned to reach about 700 by 1973. A bachelor of education degree both at the University of Nairobi and Kenyatta College was began in 1972.

The University of Nairobi grew out of the Royal Technical College and Ghandi Memorial Academy established in 1956 to provide post secondary, technical and commercial education in Kenya. Besides the common faculties, there are professional faculties of architecture, Engineering, Law, Medicine, Veterinary science, Design and Development, Agriculture, and Commercial Education. It has a School of Journalism and three institutes—the Institute of Adult Studies, the Institute of Development Studies and the Institute of African Studies.

The University awards its own degrees and has its own Grants Committee.

Commerce and Industry

At no time in the history of Kenya have so many developments on so vast a scale taken place as has been the case since the attainment of independence nearly ten years ago. These developments are not confined to a few sectors as they are many sided and encompass the entire socio-economic field. The magnitude of these achievements if viewed in the proper perspective will show that the nation has been making striking progress in the fascinating task of raising the living standards of the common man through the process of balanced development and expansion. This has brought about considerable transformation and diversification in the country's economy, the results of which are increasingly becoming manifest in different directions all over the country.

A significant feature of this overall development is the expansion and establishment of many basic and key industries which are essential for the maintenance of the nations' economy. Whereas, the substantial portion of investment has been directed towards the development of the infrastructure the Government has undertaken in conjuction with the private sector the promotion of industries to achieve an accelerated growth within the context of the Government's policy of increased industrialisation. A mixed pattern of industrial ex-

The City of Nairobi with Kenyatta Conference Centre in the background.

pansion and diversification has been adopted by working along with private enterprise so as to ensure competitive efficiency. Whereas consumer and semi-consumer and processing industries have been promoted in many cases with encouragement and participation with the private sector, all possible encouragement has been provided by the Government to develop labour intensive industries alongside capital intensive industries.

Trading activities in the domestic as well as in the foreign markets have increased and vigorous attempts have been made to ensure that Kenyans increasingly participate in this expansion of activities. These developments are visible in every sphere of economic activity, especially in the country's increasing role in the operations of the East African Community. The result of these vivid developments is the increase of the gross domestic product which stood at K£330 million in 1964 to K£835 million in 1974. The share of manufacturing in the gross domestic product has risen from K£34 million in 1964 to K£118 million in 1974, showing a cumulative rate of growth of approximately 13.2%. The contribution of wholesale and retail trade has also increased from K£32 million in 1964 to K£81 million in 1974, showing a cumulative rate of growth of approximately 10%. The growth of banking, insurance and real estate which has a direct bearing on the total amount of trade and industrial activities in the country has more than doubled from K£10 million in 1964 to K£33 million in 1974 portraying a cumulative rate of growth of approximately 13%. The registration of new companies has remained steady and whereas in 1963, 12 public and 348 private companies were registered with a nominal capital of K£12½ million, the figure for 1971 was 46 public and 939 private companies with a total nominal capital of K£13 million.

Kenya's total trade with countries outside the East African Community has continued to record substantial

DESTINATION OF TOTAL EXPORTS* 1970 – 1974

	VALUE K£ '000	
	1970	1974
E.E.C. —		
United Kingdom	15,585	18,702
West Germany	6,825	17,874
Italy	1,557	4,440
France	558	1,863
Netherlands	3,799	11,445
Other	1,476	10,582
TOTAL	29,800	64,906
Other western Europe Total	6,183	11,627
Eastern Europe Total	1,943	2,993
U.S.A.	6,772	8,029
CANADA	1,877	3,328
AFRICA —		
Tanzania	14,752	19,049
Uganda	16,698	29,287
Zambia	4,292	10,913
Other	8,080	19,345
TOTAL	43,822	78,594
MIDDLE EAST —		
Iran	337	331
Other	2,048	4,297
TOTAL	2,385	4,628
FAR EAST AND AUSTRALIA —		
Australia	655	1,140
Japan	1,231	5,364
India	3,044	2,820
China (Mainland)	619	1,787
Other	2,195	10,860
TOTAL	7,744	21,970
ALL OTHER COUNTRIES	1,475	8,200
AIRCRAFTS AND SHIPS STORES	6,900	14,134
ALL EXPORTS	108,901	218,410

*Excluding gold and currency but including Re-Exports
Source: Economic Survey 1975

ORIGIN OF TOTAL IMPORTS, 1970–1974

	VALUE K£ '000	
	1970	1974
E.E.C. –		
United Kingdom	41,459	63,949
West Germany	11,197	36,193
Italy	6,185	12,396
France	5,138	12,705
Netherlands	4,100	14,372
Other	2,923	8,705
TOTAL	71,002	148,320
Other Western Europe Total	6,161	19,526
Eastern Europe Total	3,476	10,706
U.S.A.	11,906	20,788
CANADA	796	2,811
AFRICA–		
Tanzania	5,938	9,568
Uganda	10,048	3,766
Zambia	133	2,001
Other	1,700	2,134
TOTAL	17,819	17,469
MIDDLE EAST–		
Iran	8,888	36,406
Other	5,403	34,852
TOTAL	14,291	71,258
FAR EAST AND AUSTRALIA –		
Australia	1,884	2,046
Japan	15,196	40,438
India	3,104	6,480
China (Mainland)	1,213	4,186
Other	5,618	16,320
TOTAL	27,015	69,470
All other countries	576	5,718
Parcel Posts and Special Transactions	4,970	294
TOTAL	158,012	366,361

Source: Economic Survey 1975

rises with exports directed to more than 80 countries all over the world. During 1974, our exports outside East Africa stood at K£163 million with additional exports worth K£48 million directed to our partner states in the East African Community. Total imports stood at K£366 million of which K£13 million were supplied by Tanzania and Uganda. During the year 1972, our exports outside East Africa stood at K£96 million with additional K£33 million worth of exports to Tanzania and Uganda. Our total imports during the year 1972 stood at K£177 million. This compares with exports of K£51 million and imports of K£74 million in 1963.

The principal destinations for Kenya exports are the U.K., W. Germany, U.S.A., Netherlands, Sweden, India, Zambia, Canada, Finland, Japan, Italy, and Zaire.

The mainstay of our exports are primarily agricultural products with coffee, tea, meat, sisal, pyrethrum products, wattle bark extract, beans, peas, and lentils, coffee accounting for approximately 30% of our total exports. The range of products entering export trade is increasingly diversifying with processed and manufactured goods entering into this activity.

Liberal trading policies are followed with the Majority of imports and exports on an Open General Licence (O.G.L.). However, specific import or export licences are required for certain categories of goods which are scheduled under the appropriate regulations under the imports, exports and Essential Supplies Act. A large category of items require Foreign Exchange Allocation Licence issued by the Central Bank of Kenya.

In the international economic sphere, Kenya has participated vigorously in the meetings of the Contracting Parties to General Agreement on Tariffs and Trade (GATT), the First, Second and Third Sessions of the United Nations Industrial Development Organisation, meetings of the Economic Commission for Africa and the Commonwealth Secretariat on the trade matters.

To date several bilateral trade agreements have been concluded with the socialist and African countries. These include the Republic of Egypt, Iraq, Yugoslavia, Czechoslovakia, Poland, U.S.S.R., Bulgaria, Rumania, Hungary, People's Republic of China, Swaziland, Zaire, Liberia, Sudan and the Federal Republic of Germany. In addition, we have also concluded through the East African Community an Association Agreement with the European Economic Community.

The Kenya National Trading Corporation (State Trading Corporation) was established in 1965 and undertakes a wide range of commercial activities including importation, warehousing and wholesaling. The principal aim of the Corporation is to assist in the expansion of trading activities with particular reference to the Kenyanization of the trading sectors. The Corporation has about 1,250 agents scattered all over the country distributing more than 50 commodities. The total business of these agents is in the assess of K£50 million a year.

In the decade of Independence, the rate of consumption of various commodties has increased indicating the expansion of the monetary scale of the economy and the general welfare of our people. For example, the consumption of motor spirit increased from 159 million litres in 1963 to well above 300 million litres in 1974. Electricity rose from 393 million K.W.H. in 1963 to 925 million K.W.H. in 1974. The demand for wheat flour rose from 52,000 tons to 128,000 tons in 1974; wholemilk sales from 76 million litres to 160 million litres; sugar consumption from 96.6 thousand tons to 235 thousand tons in 1974.

The effect of post independence developments has been the setting up of a number of new industries and there are at the present time more than 800 manufacturing enterprises of different types and sizes located all over the country. More than half of the manufacturing sector is based on processing of primary agricultural products. The manufacture of cement for export and local consumption is important and in addition, there are industries producing garment textiles and allied products, light engineering items, and a large range of food products. Other industries include the production of beverages, wood, furniture and paper, leather, rubber and chemicals.

The overall policy of industrialisation aims at raising the standards of living, skills and experience of Kenyans by providing employment and training opportunities. It is also aimed at providing consumers with goods and services as well as the means by which the value of the country's resources can be raised by way of processing and manufacturing. Whereas the industrial sector depends mainly on private investment in the form of equity or loan capital and other credits from within the country and outside the Government participates in the industrialisation process through industrial finance institutions such as the Industrial and Commercial Development Corporation and Development Finance Company of Kenya.

The policy can therefore, be termed as basically positive and non-restrictive, characterised by encouragement and support where needed in order to secure a maximum rate of economic growth and establishment of infrastructure which will sustain further development. Private investment is therefore, welcome not only for the capital it brings with it, but also for the transfer of modern technology, managerial and technical skills that it facilitates.

Each industrial investment proposal therefore, is viewed at with a view to satisfying the criteria related to the savings of foreign exchange, employment potential, degree of vertical and horizontal integration and decentralization of industry, to cover the whole country. Industrial incentives have been devised to promote planned industrial development and rights of ownership are guaranteed in the Constitution as well as through the Foreign Investment Protection Act. Furthermore, Kenya is a signatory to the International Investment Disputes Convention.

The promotion of small scale industries in rural areas is a priority sector for which a substantial sum has been set aside.

The Industrial and Commercial Development Corporation operates various schemes in its assistance in the development of industrial and commercial activities in the country. It is the Government's principal institution for extending credits and extension service to industrial and commercial enterprises. The corporation besides providing equity and loan capital to medium and large sized industrial and mining ventures has also set up the Kenya Industrial Estates Ltd., which already operates an Industrial Estate in Nairobi in its planned programme for developing five such industrial estates in the major industrial locations in the country.

Nairobi continues to be the chief industrial centre in the country and is also the commercial hub in the Eastern African Sub-region as it houses headquarters of many industrial and commercial organisations operating throughout the sub-region. Among the more important established industries in Nairobi are brewing, soft drinks, flour milling, pharmaceuticals, small textile and knitwear factories, cigarettes manufacture, clothing and foodstuff manufacturing, light engineering, railway workshops, and soap making. A new tyre factory has been constructed. There are also meat and fruit canning factories, a shoe factory, a sisal and rope factory, timber mills, coffee milling and processing factories, a tanning factory, cement factory and a textile factory a few miles from Nairobi. A new paper mill is now fully operational at Webuye in Western Kenya.

Mombasa has also a big industrial complex with the Port itself having ship repairing facilities. The biggest oil refinery in East

Africa is situated at Mombasa.

Other industrial centres with several small and medium sized industries are Nakuru, Kisumu, Eldoret and Thika. Industrial activities in these towns are increasing, especially with the expansion of Industrial Estates planning for such towns as Nakuru, Mombasa, Kisumu and Eldoret.

Kenya has a small but growing mining industry, producing minerals and mineral products to the value of K£4.22 million in 1974. Soda Ash continues to be the most important mineral in value terms fetching over K£2.2 million in 1974. Mineral exploration for gold, diamonds, oil and natural gas, copper, lead, and zink is in progress in various parts of the country and the use of minerals in local industry is now becoming more important. There have been significant developments with regard to some of these, notably flourspar, zinc, lead and silver. Flourspar is being mined in the Kerio Valley in the Rift Valley while zinc, lead and silver have been found in significant quanties at Kinangoni in the Coast.

Health

The Government of Kenya, through its Ministry of Health is responsible for providing good health and medical care services throughout the country. Some of the larger municipalities are also able to employ their own Medical Officers of Health and to run public health and environmental health services as well as outpatient clinical services in the form of health centres and dispensaries within their boundaries. Nairobi City Council runs one of the largest maternity hospitals in the country.

Kenyatta National Hospital on its new site is the largest and best equipped Government hospital in Kenya and functions as a referral hospital for complicated cases from the whole of the Repulic as well as the Univeristy undergraduate and postgraduate teaching hospital. Registered nurses and numerous other para medical training courses are also conducted in this hospital. This is one of the most advanced hospitals in Africa, containing all the usual clinical specialities as well as a Radiotherapy Unit and a modern Intensive Care Unit.

Each one of the seven provinces has a Government run Provincial General Hospital with the necessary specialised departments to be able to supervise and undertake the public health services and clinical care of patients in the respective province.

Each one of the numerous rural Districts has at least one government hospital generally manned by a Medical Officer of Health and general duty medical doctors. Each district has several health centres capable of dealing with common minor conditions and surveillance of the health of the community, as well as disseminating health education.

These Government hospitals and maternity services are augmented by a number of Church hospitals mainly in the rural areas, and other fee paying private hospitals which together provide around 38% of the total hospital bed capacity. There are also private medical practitioners, the majority of whom have their practices in the larger towns. There are a number of good private hospitals in the larger towns such as in Nairobi, Mombasa, Nakuru, Nyeri and Kisumu.

Mobile Health Units serve parts of the rural areas where the population is scanty and nomadic.

This service is augmented by voluntary organisations such as the Flying Doctor Service, the Wings for Progress and a Mission hospital flying health service in the remote north west of the country.

Since Kenya's independence the Government has committed considerable attention and resources towards the betterment of the health of the community and their environment emphasis being placed on promotive and preventive measures as well as the training of medical personnel. Epidemics of various diseases which used to be common in the past are no longer in evidence. Malaria has been put under control in most towns, although it is advisable for visitors from non-malaria areas to take the usual precautions. Piped water provided in many towns and game lodges is safe for drinking but hygienic precautions should be taken in the use of water from open wells and rivers. Swimming should also be avoided in dams and streams particularly in the warmer parts of the country. Swimming pools in hotels and lodges are maintained at the highest hygiene standards.

Visitors to Kenya are required to have international certificates of immunisation against smallpox and yellow fever. Immunisation against cholera is required for travellers from countries where cholera is endemic.

Money and Banking

The unit of currency in Kenya is the Kenyan Shilling, which is divided into 100 cents, with 20 Kenya shillings equal to one Kenya pound (K£). On February 16, 1973 the value of the Kenya shilling was fixed at KShs. 301.586 equal to one ounce of gold. Calculated on the basis of per value, the U.S. dollar is for the moment equivalent to Ksh. 7.14. The E.A. Central Banks however, due to the fluctuations in the money markets, declared a central rate of Shs. 7 to 1 U.S. dollar on March 13, 1973. Kenya has had no fixed relationship with the pound sterling since the sterling floated in June 1972.

Currency notes of the Central Bank of Kenya are circulated in the following denominations:— Kshs. 5, 10, 20, 100. Coins are in denominations of 5 cents, 10 cents, 50 cents and Shs. 1. The five cents and the ten cents coins are minted in nickle-brass. All the Others are cupro-nickle.

CENTRAL AND COMMERCIAL BANKS

One of the principal means available to the Government to influence the direction taken by the economy is its control over the supply of money and credit. By directing the allocation of money to give preference to particular industries or particular forms of credit, the Government can influence the rates of growth of those sectors, and of the particular forms of credit used. Control over the volume of money and credit is exercised through the Central Bank of Kenya and the 11 Commercial banks now operating in the country.

The Central Bank of Kenya was set up by an Act of Parliament on 24th March, 1966 and formally established on 23rd May, 1966 with an authorised capital of Kshs. 26 million. Its activities are governed by a board of directors consisting of a governor, a deputy governor, four other directors appointed by the President for a term of four years. The Permanent Secretary to the Treasury is appointed as an ex-officio director.

Of the 11 commercial banks, four are locally incorporated: the Commercial Bank of Africa Ltd., the Co-operative Bank of Kenya Ltd., the Kenya Commercial Bank Ltd., and the National Bank of Kenya Ltd. The remaining seven are branches of foreign banks; Algemere Bank of Baroda, Bank of India, Barclays Bank International Ltd., Grindlays Bank International (Kenya) Ltd., Habib Bank (Overseas) Ltd., and the Standard Bank Ltd.

Perhaps the most important recent development in commercial banking has been the Government's acquisition on 8th December, 1970 of 60% of the shares in the Kenya Commercial Bank which took over the local branches system of the National and Grindlays Bank Ltd. In addition, Government acquired a 40% share interest in Grindlays Bank International (Kenya) Ltd. Further, Government has indicated its wish to participate in the activities of Barclays Bank International (Kenya) Ltd. and the Standard Bank Ltd. after these two banks are incorporated locally which, together with its existing bank interests, will provide

Government with a financial stake in the greater part of banking activity in Kenya.

One of the main reasons why the Government of Kenya has wished to participate financially in the commercial banking system has been to influence the lending operations of the banks in accordance with the Government's own development policies; in particular, in accordance with the wish to encourage rural lending and lending for small-scale African enterprises.

The Central Bank acts as banker to the Government and as the administrating agent of the national debt. The Central Bank is also responsible for the implementation of exchange control with the assistance of the commercial banks. Until 1965, exchange control over capital transactions applied only to transactions with countries outside the sterling area, and within the sterling area funds were freely convertible and transferable. However, as a result of a substantial and steady foreign exchange drain to other parts of the sterling area, exchange control was, in 1965, extended to capital transactions with all countries except Uganda and Tanzania. Current transactions with all parts of the world are still only subject to minimal control designed to ensure that foreign exchange is used legitimately for the purpose stated. Since 1965, control over foreign exchange for capital transactions has enabled foreign exchange to be conserved in the country and used for national development. Even after exchange control was extended to sterling area, capital flows within the East African Community were exempted. However, when Uganda felt obliged to introduce exchange control restrictions against Kenya and Tanzania in May, 1970, quickly followed by Tanzania, Kenya was obliged to follow suit and apply capital controls within the Community in March, 1971. Effectively therefore, exchange control over capital transactions extended to all countries without exception from that date. In addition, restrictions were placed in March, 1971

Passenger train at Nakuru.

on the transfer of Kenya currency into and out of Kenya.

Communications

ROADS: Most of the road network in Kenya was originally developed in a subsidiary role to the railroad, particularly to the main line from Mombasa to Uganda. The first deliberate efforts to improve the road system began as late as 1959.

Roads in Kenya belong either to the "Classified" or to the "Unclassified" networks. The July, 1972 classified network totals about 47,500 kilometres and is made up of about 23,000 kilometres of International, National, Primary and Secondary Roads, and about 24,300 kilometres of minor roads. In addition, there are about 4,800 kilometres of unclassified special purpose roads serving tourist, tea collection, settlement and sugar areas. The length of paved roads has quadrupled in the last decade, totalling about 3,680 kilometres in 1974 and the remainder consists of gravel and earth roads.

The "Unclassified Network", composed mostly of unimproved tracks and paths, comprises a total of about 100,000 kilometres. Private Cars and Public service vehicles are used for normal motoring. Four wheel drive vehicles are required only in the remote areas.

Kenya's Development Plan 1974-78 provides for an expenditure of about K£134.5 million (or US dollars 376.6 million) at 1974 rates for capital investments for the construction and maintenance of classified network.

The Development of Trunk roads will be carried out at a total estimated cost of about K£27,240,000 (or US dollars 76,272,000) while primary, secondary and minor roads will cost K£60,305,000 (US dollars 168,854,000). Maintenance of classified roads will cost about K£47,000,000 (or US dollars 131,600,000).

In addition to this amount, a total of K£24.5 million (or US dollars 68.6 million) is earmarked for the construction and improvement of the unclassified, special purpose or service roads.

RAILWAYS: There are 1,287 route miles of railway operated by the East African Railways Corporation in Kenya. Steam and diesel locomotives are used, the former being all oil-burning. The railways also own Kisumu Port which has the main marine base on Lake Victoria with workshops and dry dock for the biggest vessels operating on the Lake. In 1973 the Railways worked goods traffic amounting to 2,715 million tons-miles.

SHIPPING: Mombasa is the largest port in East Africa serving not only Kenya but also Uganda and parts of Northern Tanzania and Eastern Congo. There are 13 deep-water berths with 2 possible container berths under construction and lighterage facilities together with an oil jetty for the modern larger tanker and a new truck cement berth. In 1971, 1,844 ships called, and total dead-weight of 7,294,725 metric tons was handled. Kenya in partnership with Eastern African countries have established a national shipping line which has been in operation for over five years.

CIVIL AVIATION: East African Airways is the Flag Carrier of East Africa and is wholly owned by the Partner States of the East African Community comprising Kenya, Uganda and Tanzania. The Airline was established in January 1946 and is one of the four Corporations of the East African Community. Its headquarters are situated in Nairobi, Kenya.

East African Airways operates a comprehensive network on the domestic routes linking Kenya, Uganda and Tanzania.

Nairobi is the main international airport in East Africa and other international airports are Dar es Salaam, Entebbe, Mombasa and Kilimanjaro.

East African Airways also operates regional and international services to Addis Ababa, Aden, Athens, Blantyre, Bombay, Bujumbura, Cairo, Copenhagen, Frankfurt, Karachi, Kigali, Kinshasa, London, Lourenco, Marques, Lusaka, Mauritius, Mogadishu, Rome, Seychelles, Tananarive and Zurich.

The East African Airways fleet consists of 4 Super VC10s, 3 DC9s, 4 Fokker Friendships and 5 Dakotas. Total revenue for the year 1974 was Shs. 559.08 million.

During the year 1974 East African Airways' aircraft flew over 105.61 million revenue passenger kilometres and carried a total of 651,050 passengers. Nairobi Airport, one of the most modern and busiest in Africa is used by 22 world airlines and its runway is 13,500 feet in length and its navigation and landing aids, including radar, 1LS, VOR and VASI can accept any commercial aircraft all over Kenya. Wilson Airport, Nairobi is the major light aircraft centre in E.A. and currently one of the busiest in Africa and the Commonwealth.

People relax on the shores of Lake Naivasha

POSTS AND TELECOM-MUNICATIONS COR-PORATION: The East African Posts and Telecommunications Corporation is responsible for the provision of postal and telecommunications services in Kenya. In Kenya there are nine Head Postmasters controlling nine Divisions, namely Nairobi, Mombasa, Nakuru, Kisumu, Eldoret, Nyeri, Kericho, Machakos and Kakamega. The total number of Post Offices in operation during the year ending 31st December, 1974 were 107 full Departmental Post Offices and 399 Sub Post Offices. The Head Post Office in the towns offer a full range Postal facilities and are supplemented by Branch Post Offices to serve effectively and efficiently the ever growing population and demand for services in such towns.

The city of Nairobi alone has 17 Branch Post Offices in addition to the main one in the city centre. Recently one new Branch Post Office has been established within the city, namely Kenyatta Hospital and at the same time arrangements are progressing well to establish three more Branch Offices in Nairobi at City Square, Nairobi South, Ronald Ngala Street and Mathare Valley. During the year ending December, 1974 72,141 private letter boxes were installed in Kenya Post Offices. Out of these, 24,538 were installed in the city of Nairobi.

Both surface and airmail services to and from all parts of the world are available. The method of delivery of mail is through private boxes, Private Bags and 'Poste Restante' for persons visiting the country who have no fixed address or local residents who do not own private boxes.

The demand for telephones between 1971 and 1974 rose by $26\frac{1}{2}\%$, and there were 17,332 people on the waiting list. The demand for telex services has also been high with an annual increase of 48%. The demand for this service has not been fully satisfied and there are always people waiting for connection.

By the end of 1974 there were 48 automatic exchanges serving 85% of the expected 49,989 total working exchange connections.

Since 1964, the responsibility for the operation of external telecommunications of East Africa was vested in the East African External Telecommunications Company Limited. The company is a wholly East African owned subsidiary of the East African Posts and Telecommunications Corporation.

In recent years East Africa has become a major international switching centre handling not only inward and outward bound East African traffic but also the traffic of its neighbouring countries. This has precipitated` great expansion and a costly modernisation programme.

The Longonot Earth Satellite Communications Station, which was built at the cost of Shs. 30,000,000/– is situated in the Rift Valley Province, some 70 kilometres from Nairobi. It provides high grade telephone links to and from East African States as well as telegraph and telex circuits. The erection of the Earth Station has resulted in high degree of efficiency by providing instantaneous telecommunications connection between East Africa and the rest of the world.

Electricity

Electricity is supplied by the East African Power and Lighting Company Ltd., (E.A.P. & L.) and the bulk supply companies, the Kenya Power Company Ltd. and the Tana River Development Company Ltd. The Power Companies operate under exclusive 50-year bulk supply licences granted by the Government.

Although the main role of the E.A.P & L. is the distribution of electricity to consumers, it owns and operates thermal generating plants and a few hydro-electric stations and transmission lines, as required, in the central and west Kenya areas, as well as three thermal power stations to supply the coast area. The E.A.P. & L. is a public limited liability company whose registered office is in Nairobi. Total issued and paid-up share capital as of 31st December, 1971 amounted to K£9.7 million and the Government has a controlling shareholding interest of over 51 per cent of the capital.

The Kenya Power Company generates and purchases electricity which it sells in bulk to E.A.P. & L. at "ascertained cost". The Kenya Power Company is a public limited liability company, which is wholly owned by the Kenya Government.

The Electric Power Act enables the Minister for Power and Communications to control by licence, consent or otherwise many important matters of company policy. For example, no increase in electricity tariffs can be effected without the approval of the Minister. This enables the Minister to ensure that tariff structure is consistent with the Government's Development Plan.

As a means of providing electricity to the rural areas, the E.A. Power Company spends at least 1% of its annual profit in what is commonly known as amenity scheme. The Company in consultation with the Kenya Government has prepared a programme of rural electrification and the implementation of the plan is expected to be accelerated as a result of financial arrangements which have been reached between the Kenya Government and the Swedish International Development Agency.

The Programme for rural electrification has been decided on the general principle of "least loss" basis on a two-tier system so that populated areas which can easily be connected to the company's existing system will be given a supply before the more remote areas, while at the same time, isolated centres of population will be fitted into the programme, so that schemes with the least loss will come first.

In order to be able to cope adequately with the increased demand for electricity supply in the country, the Company in consultation with the Government is looking for other sources of supply of electric energy. Investigations on the possibility of exploiting geothermal energy in the Rift Valley for electric power generation are in hand. Should this prove successful and show that the resources can be economically exploited, development will be embarked upon without delay. The power thus generated will be connected to the Uganda/Nairobi Transmission line for distribution throughout the country. The above exploration is being undertaken with the assistance of the United Nations Development Programme.

Employment

Wage employment in Kenya falls into three main groups; the "Modern" sector namely all known establishments in urban areas which include large scale farms, large scale enterprises (such as saw mills, sugar factories and mines) located in the rural areas and the public sector.

Two other areas of employment are the "informal" sector and the small holdings in the rural areas. The "informal" sector comprises the small individual or family concerns (mainly vehicle repairs, all types of kiosks, carpenters, tinsmiths etc). The size of this sector in terms of employment is estimated to be fairly big—though no enough research has been carried out in this area. The Government is, however, committed to assist and promote this sector as it offers gainful employment to very many people besides providing goods and services for many who cannot afford the high prices which are characteristic of the "formal" sector.

The small holdings also provide plenty of gainful employment not only to members of the families but also to numerous other locally hired labour. Shortage of hired labour is, these days, characteristic of the districts where small holder agriculture is developed, particularly in areas where tea, coffee and rice are grown by small holders. Details of wage employment in these small holdings are shown below for the period between 1969 to 1971. No details for the subsequent years are available.

The breakdown of employees by citizenship shown below shows the decline in jobs held by non-citizens to be 2.6 per cent in 1973 as compared with 3.6 per cent in 1972. The decline is a result of permanent emigration.

WAGE EMPLOYMENT IN THE ECONOMY, 1969 – 1973 ('000)

	1969	1970	1971	1972	1973	Per cent in total 1970	Per cent in total 1971
The "Modern" sector	627.2	644.5	679.7	719.6	761.6	60.6	60.9
Small Holdings	364.4	329.9	342.3			31.0	30.6
Rural Non-Agricultural Activities	81.7	90.0	95.0			8.4	8.5
	1072.3	1064.4	1117.0			100.0	100.0

WAGE EMPLOYMENT BY CITIZENSHIP: 1972 AND 1973 ('000)

	CITIZEN		NON CITIZEN		TOTAL	
	1972	1973+	1972	1973+	1972	1973+
Africans	677.1	728.6	4.4	3.5	681.5	732.1
Asians	15.2	12.1	10.0	7.9	25.2	20.0
Europeans	1.7	1.5	11.4	8.1	13.1	9.5
TOTAL	694.0	742.2	25.8	19.5	719.8	761.6
Per Cent in Total	96.4	97.4	3.6	2.6	100.0	100.0

+ Provisional

49

EARNINGS: Details of earnings in major sectors are shown below. These figures show that total earnings from wage employment in the "Modern" sector went up by K£25.3 million between 1972 and 1973, an increase of 12 per cent. During the same period, the numbers employed rose by only 6 per cent. This was most significant in the public sector, where earnings rose by 16 per cent and numbers employed by merely 4 per cent. Even within the public sector, it was recorded that earnings in parastatal bodies rose by 34 per cent in 1973 while the numbers employed rose by 7 per cent.

EARNINGS BY MAJOR SECTOR 1970-73 *(K£ MILLION)*

	1970	1971	1972	1973
Private Sector — Agricultural & Forestry.	13.7	15.1	18.6	20.6
Rest of Private Sector	75.6	82.4	88.7	96.5
Total Private Sector	89.3	97.5	107.3	117.1
Public Sector	79.3	90.6	99.5	115.01
TOTAL	168.6	188.1	206.8	232.1

TRADE UNIONS: There are 40 registered employees trade unions in Kenya. 28 of these with a combined membership of 209,184 are affiliated to the Central Organisation of Trade Unions C.O.T.U. (K) which was registered on 17th January, 1966. There are in addition 15 employers trade unions. The employers' unions are members of the Federation of Kenya Employers (F.K.E.), which was registered on 29th January, 1966.

For the purpose of the settlement of trade disputes and matters relating thereto the Government has established an Industrial

On this coastline are resort towns which cater for visitors from far afield; good hotels are situated right on the beach. Big game fishing, surfing, goggling and the full range of aquatic sports are the main attractions; there is gay, informal life and the towns have unique appeal.

Inland are the great plains of Africa, the country of game and adventure. Vast areas of the country have been set aside as National Parks, game Reserves and sanctuaries, where an infinite variety of African fauna and flora can be seen, studied and photographed in their natural habitat. Luxurious game lodges are set in the forest and mountain parklands and at dramatic vantage points in the open Savanah country, the home of countless plains game; a home of other African beasts of prey and of fascinating bird life.

The Rift Valley runs through the country from north to south, holding on its floor a number of fresh and alkaline lakes of unique interest to naturalists. Lake Nakuru is acknowledged to be one of the world's greatest attractions for ornithologists. Lake Turkana, the jade of sea and the largest alkaline Lake in the world, lies almost wholly in Kenya. Around it can be found traces of prehistoric men and extinct animals.

The Natural Resources of this country,—its wildlife which offers such an attraction to visitors from all over the world; the beautiful places in which these animals live; the mighty forests which guard the water catchment areas so vital to the survival of man and beast—are priceless heritage for the future.

The evolution of tourist industry in recent years is a good example of the role the government has assumed in the promotion of economic growth. It has pursued a policy of active involvement in all aspects of the industry, including planning and policy formulation, the setting up of standards, the creation of infrastructure, direct participation in the development of hotel and other facilities and the promotion of Kenyanization.

New activities have been initiated to sell Kenya abroad. These include the setting up of overseas tourist offices of which there were formerly 4 and now a new one has been opened in Paris with a hope of opening others in Toronto, Chicago, Los Angeles and Zurich in the near future. The game Department has been strengthened and new national parks and game reserves opened. Both to exploit a natural asset and also in the interest of conservation.

Much of the development of hotels has been undertaken by private enterprises, with or without public participation. The government has concentrated on major investments of an infracture nature without which the natural attractions of the country cannot be properly exploited. Such infrastructure includes roads, airports and landing strips.

A new tourist road connecting Lake Magadi and Mara is planned to permit development of the Nguruman area, creating a new south-west Kenya Tourist Circuit of an area which contains many cultural and scenic attractions and when ready will complement the existing Southern Kenya—Tanzania circuit.

The Total visits shown in the following tables also include Uganda, Tanzania, Zambia and other African countries.

Tourist trade has recently not met expectations due to reasons well known: the monetary crisis, decline in employment and social uncertainty in the countries of tourist origin.

By the end of 1973, there were indications of a recovery in tourist traffic inspite of the impact of the oil crisis and resultant slower economic growth around the world.

National Parks

Kenya has set aside certain areas exclusively for conservation of wildlife. These areas are administered as laid down in the National Parks Act, and they comprise:– Nairobi

TOURIST TRAFFIC 1966 – 1974

YEAR	TOTAL VISITS DEPARTURES	TOTAL DAYS STAYED '000	AVERAGE LENGTH OF VISIT DAYS	TOTAL EXPENDITURE K£ MILLION
1966	188.7	2079	11.0	14.3
1967	225.5	2327	10.3	14.7
1968	257.1	2440	9.5	17.3
1969	276.0	2352	8.5	16.7
1970	338.8	2973	8.8	16.7
1971	399.7	3734	9.3	24.1
1972	428.4	4768	11.1	27.3
1973	388.1	4435	11.4	24.3
1974	379.6	4406	11.6	26.5

VISITOR DEPARTURES BY COUNTRY OF RESIDENCE, 1972 – 1974

THOUSANDS

COUNTRY	HOLIDAY			BUSINESS			TRANSIT			TOTAL		
	1972	1973	1974	1972	1973	1974	1972	1973	1974	1972	1973	1974
United Kingdom	40.2	38.3	36.8	6.9	6.8	6.4	5.0	3.9	2.6	52.1	49.0	45.8
West Germany	34.6	32.2	31.6	1.9	1.9	2.0	2.6	2.2	1.3	39.1	36.3	34.9
Italy	11.8	13.5	16.2	1.0	1.0	1.1	1.0	1.3	1.0	13.7	15.8	18.4
France	8.4	- 9.0	9.2	0.8	0.9	0.9	0.6	0.7	0.4	10.0	10.5	10.5
Switzerland	15.6	17.7	19.7	0.8	0.9	0.8	0.7	0.7	0.5	17.0	19.2	21.0
Other Europe	20.2	22.8	27.9	2.3	2.5	2.4	2.5	2.5	1.7	25.0	27.8	31.9
TOTAL EUROPE	130.8	133.4	141.4	13.7	13.9	13.5	12.3	11.3	7.5	156.7	158.6	162.4
United States	57.9	45.4	41.5	3.3	3.7	3.1	3.4	2.9	1.8	64.7	52.0	46.4
Canada	5.6	5.1	5.5	0.5	0.5	0.5	0.6	0.5	0.4	6.6	6.1	6.4
TOTAL N. AMERICA	63.5	50.4	47.0	3.8	4.2	3.6	4.0	3.4	2.2	71.3	58.1	52.8
India	6.0	4.5	5.0	0.8	0.6	0.6	2.1	1.5	1.3	8.9	6.6	7.0
Japan	3.2	3.9	4.2	0.9	1.1	0.9	0.8	0.8	0.4	4.8	5.8	5.6
Israel	2.1	1.5	0.9	0.3	0.2	0.1	0.6	0.4	0.1	3.0	2.1	1.2
Other Asia	4.9	5.1	6.2	0.7	0.9	0.8	1.2	1.1	1.2	6.7	7.1	8.1
TOTAL ASIA	16.1	15.0	16.3	2.7	2.8	2.5	4.7	3.7	3.1	23.5	21.5	21.9
Uganda	30.4	14.1	18.5	6.0	7.3	7.6	3.5	1.8	1.5	39.9	23.3	27.6
Tanzania	74.5	63.1	51.4	10.6	9.4	10.1	6.6	5.2	3.8	91.7	77.8	65.3
Zambia	6.4	7.8	8.6	1.2	1.1	1.5	3.6	3.5	2.8	11.1	12.3	12.8
Other Africa	17.6	19.5	20.8	3.7	4.3	4.0	5.7	5.8	4.5	27.0	29.7	29.3
TOTAL AFRICA	129.0	104.6	99.3	21.3	22.1	23.2	19.4	16.3	12.5	169.7	143.0	135.0
Australia and New Zealand	3.9	3.6	4.2	0.4	0.3	0.3	0.7	0.5	0.4	4.9	4.5	4.9
All other Countries	1.8	1.9	2.1	0.2	0.4	0.2	0.2	0.2	0.1	2.2	2.4	2.5
TOTAL OTHER	5.6	5.5	6.3	0.6	0.7	0.6	0.9	0.7	0.8	7.2	6.9	7.4
GRAND TOTAL	345.0	309.0	310.3	42.1	43.7	43.4	41.3	35.4	25.9	428.4	388.1	379.6

YEAR	ADULT RESIDENTS	ADULT NON-RESIDENTS	CHILDREN	OTHER	TOTAL
1971	143,463	170,007	69,871	58,481	441,822
1972	170,189	220,993	81,506	49,522	522,210
1973	226,730	235,875	116,250	62,460	641,315
1974	186,791	219,232	56,217	68,902	531,142

National Park, Tsavo National Park (East), Tsavo National Park (West), Meru National Park, Mt. Elgon National Park, Ol Donyo Sabuk National Park, Marine (Malindi) National Parks, Amboseli National Park, Marine (Kisite/Mpunguti) National Parks, East Rudolf National Park, Lake Nakuru and Saiwa Swamp National Parks.

At present there are three National Reserves under the Kenya National Parks. These are:— Marsabit, Shimba Hills and Marine National Reserves.

In addition to these there are areas which are set aside for the preservation of historical and pre-historical objects of interest which fall under the jurisdiction of the National Museums of Kenya. These are Gedi at the Coast near Malindi, Fort Jesus in Mombasa and Olorgesailie, in the Rift Valley.

The Board of Trustees of the Kenya National Parks in close consultation with the relevant Local Authorities and the Government, through the Ministry of Tourism and Wildlife are actively looking into the possibilities of gazetting new Parks elsewhere in the country, i.e. Lambwe Valley in Nyanza Province and Kiunga near Lamu in Coast Province.

Tsavo East and West National Parks which form one single unit is the largest National Park and extends for more than 8,000 square miles (20,720 square kilometres) of bush country between Nairobi and Mombasa. The vegetation consists mainly of commiphora

56

and acacia woodlands, and in the west some spectacular mountain ranges. It contains a large number of elephants and other big game.

The influx of visitors to the Parks has been specifically remarkable since Kenya's Independence. The statistical data of paying-in visitors over the last eleven years indicate that for years to come Kenya is in for an unprecedented tourist boom. Interest among residents to visit the Parks is rapidly increasing with school children, whose interest continues to be generated by the dynamic Wildlife Clubs of Kenya, having the lion's share of the local traffic to these wildlife conservation areas.

The total number of visitors to National Parks include local residents as well as tourist visitors. The statistical data of paying-in visitors indicates that a total of 441,822 visitors entered the parks in 1971, 522,210 in 1972, 641,315 in 1973 and 531,142 in 1974.

Radio and Televison

Sound Broadcasting and Television are operated under the control of the Kenya Government through the Ministry of Information and Broadcasting, and is known as the Voice of Kenya (VOK). Sound programmes for the whole country originate from the main studios in Broadcasting House, Nairobi. These are relayed from transmitting stations situated in Nairobi, Mombasa, Timboroa, Nandi Hills and Kisumu. The main languages on sound radio are English and Swahili, but programmes also go on the air in 16 vernacular languages. They are: Kuria, Kisii, Kalenjin, Teso, Luhya, Luo, Somali, Turkana, Rendille, Boran, Swahili, Kikuyu, Kikamba, Kimeru, Hindustani and Masai. Altogether the output is 385 hours per week in 18 languages.

The Government waived the payment of annual radio and television licences since the beginning of the 1970/71 financial year. There is an operating fee of KShs. 20/– for radio sets and KShs. 60/– for television sets paid once at the time of purchase.

Television was launched in Kenya in October, 1962 and although the transmission was intended to cover a radius of 25 miles of Nairobi excellent reception was being received some 90 miles away. In May, 1964, a permanent relay station was set up at Timboroa some 155 miles (248 kilometres) from Nairobi to serve Western Kenya. A television station for the Coastal area was established at Mombasa in 1969. The main languages are English and Swahili and the output is about 38 hours per week. Local programmes occupy about 70 per cent of total transmissions.

A survey carried out in 1972 shows that there are about 35,000 Television sets and 1,050,000 radio sets in use in the country and the numbers are rising steadily.

Both sound broadcasting and television by VOK incorporate programmes with the amount of advertising increasing steadily. Towards the end of 1971 and early 1972, an engineering systems survey was carried

A herd of Zebra.

Big game fishing in one of the Kenya's Lakes.

out to determine the effectiveness of present system and to propose future improvements.

Newspapers and Magazines

Kenya has a long tradition of a free and virile independent press, and today the country boasts one of the freest and most responsible presses in Africa. There are three dailies—two in English—The Standard (founded in 1902) and the Daily Nation (1961). In addition, there are several weekly, monthly and other periodicals covering a very wide range of interests and readership.

The following is a partial list of newspapers and magazines published in Kenya:—

Daily Nation:	Founded 1961.
Circulation	67,892 90 cents a copy. Friday 72,151.
Owned By:	Nation Newspapers Limited.
Editor:	G. Githii (Editor in chief, Nation Group) J. Rodrigues (Managing Editor)
Editorial Office:	P.O. Box 49010, Nairobi, Nation House.
Readership:	All walks of life.
Editorial Policy & Contents	Independent. General.
The Standard:	Founded 1902.
Circulation	Approximately 33,000 copies daily. 90 cents a copy.
Owned By:	East African Standard (Newspapers)
Editor:	F. Young.
Editorial Office:	Likoni Road, Town House, P.O. Box 30080, Nairobi.
Readership:	48% Africans, 36% European, Remainder Asians and Overseas.
Editorial Policy & Contents:	Features, News and Sports.
Brief History:	Oldest paper in East Africa; founded in 1902 in Mombasa—moved to Nairobi in 1910.
TAIFA LEO:	Founded 1960.
Circulation:	27,000 copies daily, 30 cents in Kenya.
Owned By:	Nation Newspapers Limited.
Editor:	P.O. Box 49010, Nairobi.
Readership:	All walks of life.
Editorial Policy & Contents:	Independent. General.
Brief History:	Founded late in 1960.
Africa Samachar:	Weekly.
Circulation:	10,000 weekly, Gujarati.
Owned By:	United Africa Press Kenya Ltd.
Editor:	J.T. Bhatt.
Readership:	Gujarati speaking Asian Community.
Editorial Policy & Contents:	Cultural, political, social, and relious,

sports, hygienic questions and answers beneficial to the Gujarati.

Weekly Review:
Circulation: Not yet known; Kenya 3/50.
Owned By: Stellascope Ltd.
Editor: Hilary Ngw'eno.
Editorial Office: Esso House, Mama Ngina Street.
Readership: All races.
Editorial Policy & Contents: Objective comment on current affairs.
Brief History: Founded in 1975.

Baraza:
Circulation: 55,000 copies weekly, 50 cents in Kenya. 80 cents Uganda and 60 cents Tanzania. Swahili language.
Owned By: Baraza Limited.
Editor: F.J. Khamisi.
Editorial Office: Likoni Road, P.O. Box 30080, Nairobi.
Readership: General, East Africa.
Editorial Policy & Contents: Independent, National and Moderate News, sports and Provincial News.
Brief History: Founded in 1939, first Swahili language weekly in East Africa.

Sunday Nation:
Circulation: 70,719 English language, 70 cents in East Africa.
Owned By: Nation Newspapers Limited.
Editor: J. Gardner (Managing Editor)
Editorial Office: Nation House, P.O. Box 49010, Nairobi.
Readership: All walks of life.

Editorial Policy & Contents: Independent. General.

Taifa Kenya: (Weekly):
Circulation: 70,000 Swahili language. 30 cents a copy.
Owned By: Nation Newspapers Limited.
Editor: George Buguss.
Editorial Office: Nation House, P.O. Box 49010, Nairobi.
Readership: All walks of life.
Editorial Policy & Contents: Indepent. General.
Brief History: Founded in 1959 as a newspaper.

Sikio:
Circulation: 12,000 copies per issue. Bilingual- Swahili and English. 20 cents a copy.
Owned By: E.A. Railways Corporation.
Editorial Office: Nairobi Railway Headquarters, P.O. Box 30121, Nairobi.
Readership: *Throughout E. Africa with subscribers overseas. It is sold and distributed through agents all over Kenya, Uganda and Tanzania.*
Editorial Policy & Contents: Professional and staff news-non-political. News items of local interest to the staff of the E.A.R. Corporation.
Brief History: Started as a wall sheet in July, 1955 and changed format in 1960, and was later registered as a newspaper with the G.P.O. in November, 1962.

Africa ya Kesho: Monthly.

Circulation: 8,000 copies, Kiswahili language.

Owned By: Africa Inland Church.

Editor: John Ndeti Somba.

Editorial Office: Kijabe, Kenya.

Readership: Africa.

Editorial Policy & Contents: Items of interest to man on the street and Christian and Church articles.

Brief History: Started in 1961.

East African Report on Trade & Industry:

Circulation: 2,500 copies. English language. Price 3/− per copy.

Owned By: News Publishers Limited.

Editor: Mr. Henry Reuter.

Editorial Office: P.O. Box 30339, Nairobi.

Readership: Heads of Government, Banks at Managerial level in East Africa and the world over. It is the official journal of the Kenya Association of Manufacturers.

Editorial Policy & Contents: Commercial, East Africa Economy; Industrial and Agricultural news.

Brief History: In its present form, published since January 1970, but its predecessor—The E.A. Trade & Industry was founded and published since 1954.

Kenya Coffee:

Circulation: 2,350 copies. English language.

Owned By: Coffee Board of Kenya.

Editor: S.N. Kinyua.

Editorial Office: Plantation House.

Readership: 25,400 people.

Editorial Policy & Contents: Agricultural journal non-political.

Brief History: Established in 1935.

Kenya Farmer:

Circulation: 20,000 Bi-lingual, English/Swahili. Price 75 cents.

Owned By: Agricultural Society of Kenya.

Editor: Mrs. Iris Baker.

Editorial Office: The English Press, P.O. Box 30127, Nairobi.

Readership: This official Journal of the A.S.K. is mostly read by farming community, members of the ADK, KNFU and the Ministry of Co-orporatives and Social Services and all Statutory Boards. Also available in local, Ethiopian and Zambian Book-shops. The magazine is believed to circulate beyond continental borders.

Editorial Policy & Contents: Non-political but with support of principles laid down by the Ministry of Agriculture. Information aimed at improving the farmer, his farm and technology most of which is based on farming research work.

Brief History: The Kenya Farmer (English) and Mkulima wa Kenya

(Swahili) were issued as two separate non-profit magazines since 1950 until December 1971, when both amalgamated and the Kenya Farmer today incorporates Mkulima wa Kenya.

Lengo:

Circulation:	23,000 Swahili language; price 50 cents.
Owned By:	East African Venture Company.
Editor:	Mr. Odhiambo Okite.
Editorial Office:	Mercury House, P.O. Box 72839, Nairobi.
Readership:	East African, Mainly Tanzania.
Editorial Policy & Contents:	Comment from the Christian point of view. Church news and reviews.
Brief History:	Started in 1964 under the auspices of the Christian Councils of Kenya and Tanzania.

Safari:

Circulation:	5,000 English language; Price 2/50 per copy.
Owned By:	News Publishers Limited.
Editor:	Henry Reuter.
Editorial Office:	Ghale House, P.O. Box 30339, Nairobi.
Readership:	Tourists, Agents, Naturalists, Concervationsts, Wildlife and travel enthusiastis all over the world.
Editorial Policy & Contents:	Aimed to promote interest in tourism in E. Africa.
Brief History:	Established in March, 1968.

Target:

Circulation:	20,000 copies English language. Price 50 cents.
Owned By:	East African Venture Company.
Editor:	Odhiambo W. Okite.
Editorial Office:	Mercury House, P.O. Box 72839, Nairobi.
Readership:	Mainly aimed at those of secondary school education and primary school education for Christian readers.
Editorial Policy & Contents:	Christian comment and church news. A Review paper type.
Brief History:	Started as a successor to ROCK in 1964. It has grown up in association with the Christian Councils of Kenya and Tanzania.

Kenya Export News:

Circulation:	5,000 copies, English, free.
Owned By:	Kenya Export Promotion Council.
Editor:	Henry J. Reuter.
Editorial Office:	News Publishers Limited, Box 39339, Nairobi.
Readership:	Published on behalf of KEPC who take 2,500 copies and distribute all over the world. The rest are duly entered in the "E.A. Report on Trade & Industry".
Editorial Policy & Contents:	To promote Kenya Export. Export News.

Auto News:

Circulation:	Approximately 15,000 English. Free.

Owned By:	Automobile Association of E. Africa.		Promoting Kenya's image locally and overseas.
Editor:	Mr. M.D. Gates.	*Brief History:*	Started in 1968 in its present form. Previously it was known as Kenya Today.
Editorial Office:	Fanum House, P.O. Box 40087, Nairobi.		
Readership:	As membership.		

Editorial Policy &
Contents: General information to members. House magazine.

Brief History: First published in 1953.

Joe Magazine:
Circulation: 19,000 copies per month.
Owned By: Joe Publication.
Editor: Hilary Ngw'eno.
Editorial Office: Esso House, P.O. Box 42271, Nairobi.
Readership: All walks of life.

Inside Kenya Today:
Circulation: 30,000 copies (printed) 12,000 copies sent to Ministry of Education for distribution to schools; 15,000 copies sent to Foreign Missions for free distribution and the rest sold locally at 2/— per copy. English language Ministry of Information & Broadcasting.
Owned By: Ministry of Information & Broadcasting.
Editor: W.N. Munene.
Editorial Office: Information House, P.O. Box 30025, Nairobi.
Readership: Mainly outside Kenya.

Editorial Policy &
Contents: Illustrated features relating to Kenya.

Kenya Yetu:
Circulation: 100,000 copies. Swahili language. Free.
Owned By: Ministry of Information & Broadcasting.
Editor: Publication Officer.
Editorial Office: Information House, P.O. Box 30025, Nairobi.
Readership: Mainly unsophisticated residents in remote areas of Kenya.

Editorial Policy &
Contents: Features, news and pictures.

Brief History: The magazine takes the place of the former monthly publication "Pamoja". It is now a much larger paper and printed in five colours. The first issue came out in September, 1965.

Women in Kenya:
Circulation: Limited to members of the organization and to affiliated societies. Free. English language.
Owned By: The East African Women league.
Editor: Voluntary—A member of the league is elected annually.
Editorial Office: Administered from the E.A.W.L. Bishop's Road, Nairobi by

a voluntary committee elected annually by members of the organization.

Editorial Policy &
Contents: Non-political. Reports on the activities of the E.A.W.L. and similar organizations registered in Kenya.

Brief History: Started as an annual report about 1925 and continued for thirty years when it developed into a quarterly magazine.

Kenya Nursing Journal: Twice a year.
Circulation: 3,000 copies. English language.
Owned By: National Nurses Association of Kenya.
Editor: Mr. J. Khachina.
Editorial Office: Kenyatta National Hospital—School of Nursing.

Editorial Policy &
Contents: Matters pertaining to nursing, patients, illnesses and news from Provincial hospitals.

Brief History: Established on 2nd June, 1972.

East African Industry:
Circulation: 22,000 copies. 100/– per copy. English language.
Owned By: East African Directory Co., Limited.
Editor: Editorial Board.
Editorial Office: P.O. Box 1237, Nairobi.
Readership: Businessmen throughout the world.

Editorial Policy &
Contents: General information and classified trade index.

Industry in East Africa:
Circulation: 18,500 copies. English language. Shs. 50/– per copy.
Owned By: United Africa Press Limited.
Editor: George Kimani.
Editorial Office: Tom Mboya Street, P.O. Box 1237, Nairobi.

Editorial Policy &
Contents: Industrial boost for East Africa, complete Industrial and economic survey.
Brief History: Established in 1963.

Besides the above listed publications, there are numerous specialised publications covering cultural, educational, religeous, trade and professional interests. There are also a number of vernacular publications.

Recreation

As Kenya enjoys a good all-year-round climate, the people are keen on sports and outdoor recreations. Organised sports in Kenya include athletics, football, hockey, rugby, cricket, golf

The crested cranes. Kenya is famous for its varied birdlife.

tennis, squash and netball. At the Coast there are ample facilities for swimming, big-game and underwater fishing, surf-riding and yachting. There are also several yatch clubs up-country and numerous rivers provide good sport for anglers, especially those on the slopes of Mt. Kenya and the Aberdares. Horse-racing is popular.

Hunting in Kenya is subject to licence and certain areas are open to big-game hunting on application to the Game Department, Box 241, Nairobi. Large numbers of people enjoy gamewatching and photographing wild animals in their natural surroundings in the parks and reserves.

Nairobi has a National Theatre for the presentation of plays concerts and other functions, while there is also a local repertory company. The city has a number of cinemas and most towns have their local cinemas. Several night clubs in Nairobi cater for visitors and residents alike.

Religion

Islam influenced coastal communities, including the Arabs, many centuries ago and to some extent has spread into the interior. Today it is fairly well established among the Hamitic tribes of the Northern Province, especially the Somalis.

Christian missionaries began their work in Kenya in 1844, first at the Coast and then extending inland through Kamba and Kikuyu country to the tribes in Nyanza Province. Today there are some 25 Protestant churches and missions at work in various parts of Kenya and about 15 Roman Catholic societies. Activities are co-ordinated through the Christian Council of Kenya.

Roughly two-thirds of the Asian Community in Kenya belong to various Hindu sects, while the others subscribe to Islam. There is a sizeable following of the Ismaili religion, especially in the towns. There are both Protestant and Catholic groups among the European and other smaller communities.

Immigration

Visitors' Passes are necessary for all visitors to Kenya and can be obtained from the Principal Immigration Officer, P.O. Box 30191, Nairobi or from the nearest Kenya Embassy or High Commission, or on arrival subject to the possession of a visa. Where applicable, and such other conditions as may be required by Immigration Office, visitors are advised for their own convenience to apply in advance.

Every visitor requires a valid passport (or form of international recognized travel document) properly endorsed for travel to Kenya and a Kenya visa must be obtained by all persons except the following countries: Commonwealth countries (with a few exceptions), Denmark, Norway, Italy, Spain, San Marino, Turkey, Uruguay, Ethiopia, West Germany, and Sweden.

Customs

Duty-free entitlement depends on the category of the passenger whether an immigrant, a tourist or a returning resident.

As a rule all used personal and household effects, cameras, and accessories (but not including biycles, cine or still projectors, gramophones and gramophone records, provisions, wireless and television etc.) are allowed in duty free. Exposed film, firearms and ammunitions will also be admitted duty free provided Police permits for firearms and ammunition are produced.

Items which must be declared but are admitted free of duty include ½ Lb tobacco, or equivalent in cigarettes or cigars and alcoholic liquors not exceeding one pint each. Souvenirs brought in by tourists from other counries can be declared under deposit until the passenger leaves the country again. This also includes such articles as musical instruments, radios, tape-